AFFIRMATIONS

200 Positive

FOR

Affirmations for

HAPPINESS

a Joyful Mindset Every Day

KELSEY AIDA ROUALDES

ADAMS MEDIA

NEW YORK   LONDON   TORONTO   SYDNEY   NEW DELHI

Adams Media
An Imprint of Simon & Schuster, Inc.
57 Littlefield Street
Avon, Massachusetts 02322

First Adams Media hardcover edition November 2020

ADAMS MEDIA and colophon are trademarks of Simon & Schuster.

For information about special discounts for bulk purchases, please contact Simon & Schuster Special Sales at 1-866-506-1949 or business@simonandschuster.com.

The Simon & Schuster Speakers Bureau can bring authors to your live event. For more information or to book an event contact the Simon & Schuster Speakers Bureau at 1-866-248-3049 or visit our website at www.simonspeakers.com.

Interior design by Katrina Machado
Interior images © Getty Images/ulimi; 123RF/Veronika Golovko

Manufactured in the United States of America

10 9 8 7 6 5 4 3 2 1

Library of Congress Cataloging-in-Publication Data
Names: Roualdes, Kelsey Aida, author.
Title: Affirmations for happiness /
Kelsey Aida Roualdes.
Description: Avon, Massachusetts: Adams Media, 2020.
Identifiers: LCCN 2020034496 | ISBN 9781507214473 (hc) | ISBN 9781507214480 (ebook)
Subjects: LCSH: Happiness. | Affirmations.
Classification: LCC BF575.H27 R695 2020 | DDC 158.1--dc23
LC record available at https://lccn.loc.gov/2020034496

ISBN 978-1-5072-1447-3
ISBN 978-1-5072-1448-0 (ebook)

Introduction

Ever find yourself wishing you were happier? That you could discover more delight in everyday things? That you could feel good no matter what your current circumstances and create long-term contentment? You can—with *Affirmations for Happiness.*

The truth is that happiness is not something to be found but rather something you can create! No matter how things seem to be playing out in your life, you can consciously *choose* to feel happy—unconditionally, unapologetically, and without boundary. Reciting affirmations—short, positive statements you can say aloud or to yourself that are meant to inspire change—is one effective way to create more happiness in your life.

That's right: Happiness is something you can cultivate and practice in simple ways every day. Each new breath you take is an opportunity to open your heart to happiness, embrace it more than ever before, and enjoy the abundance already in your life! Every affirmation contained in the following pages is designed to help ease you into this inspired, optimistic, and blissful state. The words will help you release the blockages that once held you back from experiencing more joy, so you will naturally find yourself feeling happier.

Reciting these words will help you own your happiness in an empowering and truly authentic way. Cultivating happiness does not mean that you have to force a fake smile or deny how you really feel. All you have to do is observe how you feel and follow the thoughts, choices, and actions that are the most empowering and joyful to you! This process will look different for everyone, which is why you'll find hundreds of options in this book—you can use the affirmations that resonate most strongly with you.

You might already have some ways to invite joy into your life—spending time with loved ones, pursuing hobbies, or enjoying the outdoors. Consider this book another helpful tool to add to your well-being tool kit for more happiness, joy, and empowerment. It will guide you through many beneficial thought patterns, beliefs, and perspectives so you can formulate a mindset that encourages joyful abundance. The moment has come to create more happiness in your life, one affirmation at a time!

How to Use This Book

More happiness is yours for the taking and this book will help you get there! The ideas, guidance, and daily reminders will give structure to your happiness journey.

Here are some suggestions to help your affirmation practice be as powerful as possible:

- **Make these affirmations a part of your daily routine.** Recite these affirmations as often as it feels good for you, and incorporate them into your life however you want—this practice is very flexible and can fit into any schedule. For example:
  - Start your day by reciting an affirmation as you take your morning shower.
  - Write affirmations down on a sticky note and post them around for gentle reminders.

- Set an alarm on your phone to help revisit certain affirmations throughout the day.
- Pick your favorite affirmation at the moment and meditate on it for a minute.
- Make the most of otherwise wasted time (on your commute, in a waiting room, etc.) to silently repeat a mantra to yourself.
- Be creative and choose a method that works for you on any given day.

Be open. The more open your mind and body are as you absorb the wisdom and medicine behind each affirmation, the better they will work for you. Practice good posture and keep your heart open as you read, contemplate, and recite these affirmations. It's helpful to always set the intention to open your mind to new perspectives before you dive into this book.

Feel free to tweak affirmations so they work for you. Try on each affirmation like you would try on a new outfit. If it doesn't quite fit, you can always tailor it to better suit you. Try using phrases like "I am learning how to..." or "I am willing to..." or "It is my intention to..." in order to soften an affirmation and make it more accessible to you in any moment.

Speak your dreams into existence by reciting your favorite affirmations out loud. You can declare these affirmations to yourself in the mirror, tell them to the universe, or even share them with a supportive friend. Putting an audible vibration behind your intentions is a surefire way to give them even more creative power!

Write them down when they speak to your soul. Writing down affirmations is another extremely powerful way to turn your intentions into your reality! Whenever an affirmation really works for you, write it out on a piece of paper or in your journal—the more slow and deliberate you are, the better. If a particular affirmation really moves you, try hand lettering it in a lovely font.

- **Use this book to help you change your outlook after you feel down.** Sometimes you'll feel sad, mad, or just plain down, and that's okay! It's always best to honor whatever you are experiencing. If these affirmations feel inauthentic when you try to practice them, that just means you're not a vibrational match to them in that moment, and that's okay too. Process whatever emotion you are going through first, then come back to this book to help you move forward with optimism and relief!

- **Practice compassion and patience with yourself.** Technically, there is no "right" or "wrong" way to practice affirmations. Focus on the options that resonate with you and your situation, and periodically revisit ones that didn't to see if anything has changed. Don't be upset if you miss a day here or there; you can always pick up where you left off anytime.

- **Try gently smiling or breathing a sigh of relief after you encounter an affirmation that works for you.** Take a moment to really integrate the medicine of the words you've just read. Let them sink into your whole being. Accept them as your new reality. Sitting with an affirmation for a few extra moments can make it even more powerful.

- **Share them with a friend!** If anyone in your life ever asks you for encouragement or support, offer them one of your favorite affirmations to help! Let them know what words have helped you, and encourage them to customize them to their heart's content.

Stick with them, and these affirmations will help you to create exponential positive change in your life over time. Here are some of the signs that these affirmations are already helping you:

- You start to feel a sense of relief.
- You become more aware of your thoughts.
- You begin embracing more joy.
- You judge your life experience less.
- You live with more gratitude and appreciation.
- Your perspective shifts to always benefit your mood.
- You just plain feel better!

First, you'll notice subtle changes in your perspective and mood, and then, before you know it, you've incrementally multiplied your happiness!

Happiness is my birthright.

Every being deserves to be happy and free,
including me. Nothing can take away this basic,
inherent right. I'm ready to finally recognize
what has always been mine! I'm stepping into
my divine worthiness starting now.

I am becoming a magnet for joy!

Today's the day! I'm consciously using my breath to make space in my body, mind, and heart to gracefully attract new levels of joy. I'm ready to welcome more joy into my experience.

Feeling good is my highest priority.

My feelings matter to me. All my feelings are valid, and I will process them with patience and grace. I will follow what feels best for me, prioritize feeling good, and love myself through the process.

It's time to
concentrate on
my happiness!

I am open to being happier than ever before.

Every moment gives me a chance to embrace a deeper level of fulfillment, joy, and gratitude. I invite these feelings in with the openness of my heart. It's time to experience more of what life has to offer.

My potential is limitless.

From now on, I'm doing my best to see the joy and abundance available to me. I let go of my self-inflicted restrictions and look for opportunities to fulfill my potential. I'm ready.

*I can always find
new opportunities
to enjoy.*

Each new day is a gift with an infinite number
of potential presents—I can choose to see
as many as I want. I can find happiness in
a wide variety of places. I choose to seize
these moments and enjoy them a little more.

*I honor the hard times
that help me appreciate
the happy ones.*

Without sadness, I would not know happiness.
Without lack, I would not know abundance.
The contrast of life is a gift. I'm no longer
labeling emotions as "good" or "bad." I see
the value in all of it.

When
I put my
attention on
good things,
I notice more
of them.

I use my imagination for positive creation.

I'm making the conscious choice to use my imagination for beneficial creation rather than for fearful projection. There's no need to waste my precious energy worrying over what might happen when I can instead channel my energy into manifesting happiness! I choose faith over fear and imagine the best.

My bliss is calling me.

Surrender carries me to bliss. Instead of focusing on outcomes, I instead imagine myself gently floating downstream, allowing life to happen. It's nice to let things work out for me. It's nice to trust my life. It's nice to feel free. All I have to do is let go.

I can love my life, even if it's not "perfect."

Happiness happens!

Happiness is a natural part of life. Happiness happens without me having to try, or force and manipulate my life or mood. Happiness happens as an inevitable by-product of gratitude, connection, and authentic expression.

I actively choose thoughts that please my mind and soothe my soul.

I'm taking responsibility for consciously choosing thoughts that serve me well. I only hold on to thoughts that are empowering. Other thoughts will still inevitably come, but I will gracefully let them go. The only truth is love. If my thoughts don't feel loving, I know they are not the truth.

Today I'm choosing happiness.

In every moment, I have the free will to
choose. I can choose to feel happy every day,
even if only for a moment. Every time
I choose how I want to feel, my emotional
muscles become stronger. I am becoming
the master of my inner world.

Feeling is healing.

Embracing every feeling is my quickest path to
long-term stability and joy—because my heavy
emotions will no longer hold me down once
I've given them the love and attention they
need in order to heal. I openly welcome all
emotions ("positive" and "negative") in order
to draw more happiness into my inner world.

I can be
happy!

*I am ready to receive
more laughter,
optimism, and joy.*

I intend to make time for play and laughter.
I intend to practice more optimism in my
thoughts. And I'm willing to be more joyful,
even if it's just slightly more than yesterday.

I give myself permission to be happy.

Today I end the search for the very thing that can only be created within. I gift myself the permission I've been waiting for—permission to be happy, unapologetically and without condition. It's okay to feel good. I'm allowed to be happy!

I focus on
what feels good
and let the rest
fall away.

I am willing to change my approach to cultivate good feelings.

I might need to alter the way I see my life in order to get new results. I will no longer go in circles living my life in the same way I always have. It's time to level up! It's time to try something new.

*It's fun to love my life
more and more every day.*

I enjoy the process of learning how to enjoy
life. Every day it gets a little bit easier as I get
a little bit more comfortable with the process.
I'm shifting my focus to look for things to love.
There are many positive aspects in my life and
I choose to acknowledge them now.

My happiness
is mine to
design.

Happiness comes naturally when I let go of what no longer serves me.

As I loosen my grip on the heaviness that holds me down, I gently float back up to the surface, where joy resides. Now weightless and without restraint, I'm ready to embrace my true nature of happily relaxing in the present instead of clinging so tightly to the story of my past.

My relationships are a source of true fulfillment and delight.

I cultivate and nourish the connections
in my life that offer me support, love,
connection, and joy. I let others fill my cup as
I fill theirs. I know that life is not meant to
be lived alone. Genuine connection is key
to my well-being.

My desires matter.

I am here to create a wonderful life for myself and those around me. I owe it to myself and the world to make the joyful visions in my mind a reality! I know my genuine desires are an important part of me and I am actively pursuing them.

*I choose to stop playing
life on hard mode.*

There's no need to make things harder than
they need to be. Life is meant to be fun,
enjoyable, and sometimes challenging—like a
good game. It might be hard at times,
but ultimately I'll have had a good time
participating!

My happiest
days are
yet to come.

I make time for happy moments throughout the day.

I'm including happiness as a part of my agenda today and every day. I consciously pencil in time to encourage happy thoughts, laughter-filled moments, and expressions of gratitude. From now on, happiness is a part of my daily self-care routine.

I craft my stories wisely and with intention.

As I become witness to my inner world, I choose only to create stories (aka: meanings I assign to events in my life) that feel good to me. I know which stories help me experience ease and happiness and which stories hurt me by how they make me feel. Self-empowerment starts in my mind and with the meanings I assign to things.

I owe it to myself to find out what makes me happy.

I'm constantly learning more about myself.
My preferences...my values...and my desires.
I want to find out more about what lights me
up so I can encourage my happiness. This will
no doubt lead me to feeling fulfilled!

I don't have to chase happiness; I only have to let it in.

There is nothing to chase and nowhere to go. My job is to open my heart, soothe my nervous mind, and let happiness come to me and through me.

It is safe to have it all.

I can expect miracles when
I embrace my highest joy.

When I am joyful, I am able to attract
miracles into my life. I'm choosing to spend
more time in this open and radiant state
for the benefit of myself and everyone
around me.

I'm always looking for something to celebrate.

Celebration is a form of praise and I like to praise what's working! It makes me feel good to notice what's going right and how blessed I truly am. I'm on the lookout for evidence of abundance, and I will find it and commemorate it.

Life flows easily when I make time to enjoy the ride.

I'm ready to claim my happiness!

There's no reason why I cannot be happy if I choose to be. Happiness is for all of us and I'm ready to claim mine starting now.

Well-being is a top priority for me.

It's my intention to make feeling good a top priority. If I have to choose between something that dampens my well-being or something that feels better, I promise to choose what feels best. My well-being matters to me and this is reflected in my choices, actions, and priorities.

I'm free to change my perspective in any moment.

I have the freedom and ability to see things in new and empowering ways whenever I feel powerless. Beneficial perspectives are always available to me when I encourage myself to see things differently. If I ever feel down or stuck, all I have to do is adjust my viewpoint!

I choose to embrace the little things that bring me joy!

It's easy for me to be happy when I recognize life's simple pleasures. All these little things eventually add up to this big thing called life. There is beauty, joy, and pleasure all around. All I have to do is take it in.

Life is really
beautiful
when I notice
everything
that's going
right.

I prioritize activities that make me happy.

If it brings me joy, it's going on the agenda! Just because I'm not a kid anymore doesn't mean I have to lose sight of fun, play, and delight. I spend time doing what I love because I can. There's no good reason to deprive myself of fun.

I'm allowed to feel good for no reason.

I don't need certain conditions in place before
I allow myself to feel good and be relaxed.
Conditional emotions are a thing of my past!
I'm allowed to embrace feeling good simply
because it feels good!

Inspiration
for bliss is all
around me.

*I'm getting better and better
at cultivating my joy.*

The more I practice being in a state of joy,
the easier it becomes for me. The more
intentional and consistent I am with this new
daily practice, the better I will feel.
My joy is growing exponentially.

When I'm happy, I give others permission to be happy too.

If I'm in a joyful state of mind, the people around me see that it's okay for them to be happy too. I love leading by example and helping people along the way.

Good food nourishes my body and supports my joy.

I take in foods that optimize my health and encourage my well-being. My healthy choices lead to a healthy mind with healthy thoughts. The more good food in my system, the easier it is to naturally feel good!

The "right time" for joy is now.

It's time for me to notice when I'm withholding my own happiness from myself. Enough is enough! It's silly to put off feeling good for another day, a different outcome, or better circumstances....All my power is in the now. Why wait?

I'm
beautiful
when I'm
smiling.

I make the most of my happy moments.

I'm not *always* happy, and that's okay. But when I am happy, I stay present and truly relish those moments! I savor this joy and that helps me manifest even more happiness for myself.

*I swiftly find peace when
I simplify my life.*

My peace is always there—it simply
gets buried underneath all the ways I
overcomplicate things. I give up this habit and
choose to simplify. There's no need to make
things harder than they need to be.
Simplicity feels good.

My life is my canvas.

My heart knows exactly where my greatest joy lies.

My heart carries a unique step-by-step map
to my personal joy and fulfillment. I'm ready
to really start listening and let it show me the
way! Whenever I'm uncertain or unclear,
I'll simply tune in and ask my heart,
"What should I do?"

I support my body in a loving way.

I do what is in my body's best interest to give myself the best possible chance at health and happiness. I sleep well, hydrate often, eat nutritiously, and move regularly. Happiness is so much easier when I make sure that all my basic needs are met!

I don't resist negativity.
I simply choose positivity
instead!

What I resist persists. Pushing against
anything is never the easiest way. Instead
of pushing against the unwanted, I simply
cultivate more of what I do want and place my
attention there. I focus with intention in the
direction I want to go.

I let my purpose lead the way to happiness.

The ideas, goals, and activities that bring me joy are directly tied to my purpose in life. To feel more fulfilled, I'll simply follow the path that matches my values and principles.

It's natural
for me to
want more
happiness.

I'm willing to release judgments in the name of joy.

I let go of all judgments of myself and my life
experience: my partner, my boss, my friends,
my family, my body, my accomplishments,
my habits, my time line, my thoughts, my
mood, my progress, my circumstances, and
ultimately my life. Constantly appraising and
rating myself only makes happiness more
difficult to create. As I let these judgments
slip away, I create space for more loving
perspectives to enter my mind.

*Happiness is never
far away.*

Sure, sometimes joy gets lost in this emotional roller coaster known as life. But no
matter how many times I lose sight of my
happiness, I can rest assured knowing that it
will always come back to me.

I can identify happiness in my past, present, and future.

My free will is a gift that I put to good use!

I always have choices. I will utilize this superpower to take whatever action is most empowering for me in that moment. I'm thankful for my ability to choose happiness!

I'm trading my worry for faith.

Worrying too much holds me back from my natural state of relaxation and contentment. I would rather try to trust and have faith, so that's what I'll do! Life is too short to stress over the little things. I'm ready to set myself free.

The beauty
of nature
affords me
so many
opportunities
for joy.

I'm already winning!

It's impossible for me to "lose" because everything that happens is for my highest good. Even when I can't see why or understand how, I choose to trust this universal truth. Everything happens for a good reason—and I can still create happiness.

I choose to thrive in joy.

It's time for me to graduate from survival mode to thriving mode! I will no longer tolerate a life of struggle. I choose to thrive in a new, more joyful experience. I'm ready to level up!

I help generate happiness by nourishing my mind.

I am kind to my mind. I give it everything it needs to function optimally for me. I think nice thoughts, I practice beneficial perspectives, I give it time to rest, and I use it as an ally on my journey toward more happiness.

I let laughter
be my
medicine.

I appreciate my blessings often.

It feels good to take note of all the blessings in my life. I'm always looking for what's going right and the things I can be grateful for. I love being in a state of appreciation. I'm so thankful for all I have.

Healing leads to my happiness.

When I'm unhappy, that's my cue that something inside me needs more love, care, or attention. My emotional healing is the foundation for my lasting happiness. I will focus on healing when my mind, body, or spirit needs it.

To receive more
happiness,
I simply give
it to others.

My furry friends bring me lots of joy.

I'm so thankful for the pets in my life that love me unconditionally and remind me to have more fun. It makes me happy to know that they will love me no matter what I'm going through. I love them for making me smile.

I appreciate the people in my life who value my happiness.

I'm thankful for the people in my life who want to see me happy. I love them for encouraging my joy. These relationships are incredibly valuable to me. I honor them and am open to having more!

Grateful
thoughts
effortlessly
create joy.

I choose happy habits.

If a habit of mine is taking away from my happiness, I can always replace it with a more beneficial one that supports my overall well-being. My habits are mine to choose with deliberate intention! I decide which habits I engage in and which I don't. I can create new positive habits anytime.

I let the light in.

I welcome the lighter, more enjoyable
experiences of life without judging the heavier,
more uncomfortable ones. No emotion is right
or wrong, better or worse. I simply choose
to spend more time feeling good than I do
anything else.

Happiness begins with me!

I no longer need to look to other people, outer
circumstances, or arbitrary milestones in order
to start feeling better. Happiness is a personal
choice that begins with a simple intention. I
am taking full responsibility for my happiness
and well-being starting now.

Joy is my true nature.

My inner self is reflected in my outer reality.

When I focus on generating happiness inside myself, I will also create that environment outside myself. I'm excited to see how my new emotional well-being will be reflected back to me by my outer reality.

I have nothing but time to practice and master my enjoyment.

I have time to keep practicing happiness.
I have time to master my well-being. I have
time to keep learning and growing. I have
time to keep improving my life. There is no
destination, only time.

My circumstances do not have to define my mood.

I treat my happiness like a fun hobby.

Happiness is not a destination for me
to "arrive at" or something for me to
"accomplish" or "achieve." My happiness is
a practice, a choice, a lifestyle...a new way of
being. I'm embracing the limitless unfolding of
my true nature and having fun along the way!

It's not about how much I have, but how much I enjoy.

Having more never leads to happiness in the ways that I hope it will. That's why I'm shifting my focus from obtaining more things to expanding my joy. All I'm really after is more enjoyment in life.

I'm opening the door to new possibilities for joy.

I'm inviting fresh energy into my life with the intention of creating something new. A new project, a new goal, a new feeling... I'm ready to freshen things up and go in a direction that truly serves me. Joyful opportunities await me!

My happiness
can look
however I
want it to.

I'm brave for changing my life in support of my happiness.

Change isn't always easy or comfortable, but I'm willing to do what it takes in order to feel better. I admire myself for having the courage to create my dream life and go after what I want.

I rejoice in the way things are.

When I can cherish the present moment—
without needing anything to change right
away—I am free to celebrate my life no matter
what! It is only natural to rejoice. After all,
there is so much to celebrate in this life.

I am the observer of my inner world.

I'm curious about what's going on inside me. Instead of judging myself for how I feel, I choose to use compassionate inquiry from now on. Why am I feeling this way? How am I doing right now? What do I need in this moment to be happy?

I am grateful to be alive!

My life and my joy are a gift and I recognize this often. I give thanks for my health, my safety, my relationships, my mission, and my passion for feeling good. I'm glad to experience this point in time.

My only
job is to
follow what
feels good.

My needs are valid.

The things that I need in order to have peace
and contentment are perfectly normal. My
needs are never wrong or "too much"; they are
the foundation for living a good and healthy
life. When my needs are met, I thrive!

I protect my happiness.

My happiness is sacred to me. To protect it from energetic interference, I call upon an impenetrable healing white light to encompass my energy field. May this light protect me while I amplify my joy from within. May I always have this blessing of light from now on.

I'm making space for more happiness in my life!

It's time to cut away the things in my life that suppress my joy to make room for more happiness to enter. Space in my home, space in my schedule, space in my relationships, and space in my mind. Happiness, come on in!

Being present helps me feel happy.

When I am present in the moment, my anxiety subsides and any worry lifts away. When I am present, I can find safety and calm. When I am present, I am fully in my power! Presence is my key to contentment.

I let grace be my guide.

Today is another opportunity for happiness.

No matter what happened yesterday, last
week, or the year before, today is a
brand-new slate. I've been blessed with yet
another chance to enjoy, play, create,
and love....Every moment is new.
I can choose joy at any time!

I'm awakening to my truth.

Whether I'm already conscious of it or not, I am awakening to my personal truth, which will always lead me to joy. I wish to become aware of what I'm truly here to do, be, and experience.

I am always living the best version of myself.

The best version of me is never lost. No matter what I've been through in the past, I can choose to live fully from this empowered state.

I can always come back to center when I'm ready.

No matter my emotional state, my center is always available to me. All I have to do is quiet my mind to find it. This is where my eternal joy lives, untouched and unwavering.

I'm choosing to feel good because I can.

When I'm happy, I experience clarity.

I use the clarity and optimism that stem from my happiness to make choices that align with my highest good. Happiness brings me clarity, and clarity shows me the most beneficial direction to go in.

*Every season brings me
happiness in its own
unique way.*

In the summer, happiness is inevitable thanks
to the lovely weather. In the fall, I let go of
whatever is keeping me from happiness. In the
winter, I heal my heavier emotions so as to
come back to happiness. And in the spring,
I birth new creations that make me happy.

Feelings of
ease and flow
are always
available to me.

I feel more and more blessed every day.

The more I look around for things to be
thankful for, the more things I find! Every
day is a new opportunity to give thanks for my
many blessings. And even when it feels like
I've run out, I know I haven't.

I embrace my carefree nature.

There is a part of me that is totally carefree. Today I choose to explore this lighter side of myself. What would it feel like to let go a little more? How much can I surrender? Where can I take a leap of faith?

I choose optimism.

I always have a choice: to look down or up, to look backward or forward. Now I will look up with hope in my eyes and forward with positive expectation in my heart. The deepest part of me knows that the best is still yet to come!

I get to be exactly as happy as I decide to be.

*I'm always finding
new and delightful ways
to experience joy.*

I'm studying myself and making a list of all
the things that help support my happiness.
Every day I'm learning what it takes to make
me happy. Knowing what I like and sticking to
my personal preferences helps!

My stream of well-being is infinite.

There is a never-ending source of well-being
that's always flowing to me and through me.
Whenever I'm not well, it's simply because
I've stepped out of my stream. I'm getting
back into my flow and allowing it to take
me to my joy.

The happiest version of me is only a few breaths away.

When I slow down my breath, I remember the truth of who I really am. I use deep breathing as a tool for accessing my joy. Ahh...

It's my time to shine.

It's time to show the world how radiant,
blissful, and expansive I can truly be. I want
to share my bright light, live out my joy,
and express my truth. Today is the day to
beam with confidence and shine brighter
than ever before.

I'm coming into alignment with my most joyful self.

I'm allowing more cheer into my life.

I'm celebrating all the good things that are available to me. I have plenty of room for more because my container for joy is limitless, just like the infinite nature of the universe.

I'm creating a blissful life.

I'm positively transforming my life by giving my attention and dedication to my hopes, dreams, and desires. I focus most of my energy on what I want to create. My thoughts are dedicated to building something even better than what I'm experiencing now.

There are so many things to be happy about!

I write down my happy moments.

I keep a journal of all the blessings in my life and happy things that happen for me throughout the day. This way I can always remember the good times and revisit them whenever I feel down. Recording my happiness helps it to live on forever.

I welcome joyful surprises and big blessings.

I am opening myself up to receive big, happy changes in my life. I am ready to take in the best of what life has to offer. I will embrace and appreciate whatever is around the corner.

I follow the feeling of relief.

My relief leads me to my greatest joy.
Whenever I'm unsure of what to think or what
to do, I simply do whatever brings me
long-term relief. Following my relief feels
good, and that's exactly what I'll do.

Today is my opportunity to build a brighter tomorrow.

I'm going to set myself up for success and pave the way for a better future. This is my chance to set the tone for the rest of my life. I'm choosing empowering thoughts and setting my hopes high. No matter what today was like, tomorrow is going to be even better!

I'm making
my life an
expression of
joy.

I'm going to be someone's sunshine today.

Bringing joy to others brings joy to me too!
Today I'm going to shine my light on anyone
and everyone who's willing to receive it.
No matter what the weather is outside, I'm
making my own sunshine everywhere I go.

Appreciating my body more often encourages my happiness.

For every "flaw" I want to change, I can find at least three things that are amazing about my body and focus on those instead. The more I acknowledge what a magical blessing it is to be healthy and alive, the happier I naturally feel. Judgment no longer has a place here. It's time to appreciate my soul's home.

I'm already on
the path
because joy is
my destiny.

I'm a collector of joy.

I like to collect joy because joy creates a lot
of great things for me. It cultivates my
resilience, my appreciation, my contentment,
my pleasure, and, of course, more joy!
Collecting joy brings me that much closer
to emotional freedom.

My life is my playground!

It's fun to imagine, build, and play. If I don't like what I've made, I can knock it down and start again. How lucky that I get to create whatever I want in this sandbox called life!

I cherish my feelings and emotions.

I'm so thankful to have the sensitive emotional compass that I do. My happiness comes easily when I follow what feels good and tend to myself when I feel bad. My emotions are constantly leading me back to my truth, my peace, and my purpose.

It is safe to enjoy my life.

Although some parts of me may be resistant
to release control, I know that I am safe
to let go and enjoy. It is safe to find pleasure
in the present moment. It is safe to stop
worrying so much. Nothing bad can come
from my enjoyment.

I am joyfully me.

I release all resistance
starting now.

I now gently release to the universe whatever
has been holding me back from experiencing
the maximum amount of joy available to me.
I'm ready to live in a state of flow, ease, and
joy. I surrender it all so that I can
feel better!

I ask for wisdom to understand more about happiness.

It's extremely enlightening for me to gain
more understanding about happiness.
I question what makes me happy. I ask others
what makes them happy. I pray that I can
really understand happiness on a deep level
so as to embody it fully.

Joy happens
to me when
I realize how
good things
really are.

I allow faith to lead me to happiness.

Even though things haven't always been easy for me, I choose to cultivate an unshakable sense of optimism from today forward. I want to know what it's like to never question my path and look forward to my future. I'm ready to deepen my faith.

I let love guide me to my joy.

All I have to do is let the light in and joy naturally finds its way to me. Love is another pillar of support for my joy, which is why I choose to practice and receive it openly and without restriction.

The ability of the universe to give me what I need humbles me.

I have faith in the power of the universe to deliver to me what I need and want better than I could ever do by myself. The universe is much more resourceful than me, so I'll set my intentions for happiness and then stay open for surprises as to how it will come!

Connection is my key to fulfillment.

I make it a point to connect with myself and others to support my joy and contentment. Connection with myself and the right people brings so much richness to my life! I'm thankful for all my valuable connections and will keep nurturing them with love.

Thriving is my
calling, and
more joy will
get me there!

I always deserve more happiness, not less.

When I'm upset, I deserve more happiness, not less. When I'm stressed, I deserve more happiness, not less. When I'm happy, I deserve even more happiness, not less.

I'm ready to experience more inner peace.

I can access my stillness in order to let happiness rise from within. There is a part of me that is always still and at ease. I want to experience this aspect of myself more often. I'm ready to befriend my peace and experience it more deeply than before.

My dreams
are attainable.

My inner joy is reflected to the world as kindness.

My joy is a blessing for all and of harm to no one. When I am truly joyful, it is received by others as kindness. Just another good reason to live more in joy!

The less I compare, the more I enjoy.

Comparison is the thief of joy, so I choose not to partake in it today. There's no need for comparison. All that really matters is that I embrace my unique journey and release any self-judgment that blocks me from truly enjoying it. It can be that simple.

I'm moving in a positive direction!

I'm improving my life and moving in a beneficial direction. I'm not concerned with my pace because I know I am on the time line that's right for me.

All my power
is in this
present
moment.

I do not rely on material goods for happiness.

Maybe happiness is less about what I have and more about supporting my emotional freedom. A clear mind and heart is where my real happiness lies.

It's empowering to keep choosing happiness.

I can feel powerful by feeling good. It's empowering to take responsibility for my life. I can do, have, be, or feel whatever I want! Nothing feels better than being in my power.

The sounds of nature help me reconnect.

If I ever need help relaxing into my peace, I can always call upon nature to guide me there. Spending time in nature, or even just enjoying the sounds of nature, unravels my nervous system so I can let more joy in. Nature is my friend, encouraging joy.

Fun is my gateway to joy.

When I'm having fun, it's easy to feel joyful
and delighted. It's about time I start letting
myself have a little more fun every day.
I give myself unapologetic permission to
have more fun.

It feels good
to let myself
enjoy.

I choose to be unreasonably happy.

I don't need reasons to feel happy. I
can be happy simply because I feel like it!
I can choose to think of reasons if I want—
there are plenty—but I don't need to justify
my happiness to anyone.

I let my intuition lead me to happiness.

The most evolved and enlightened part of me
calls me toward more joy. It communicates
to me through the whispers of my intuition.
It knows exactly where I want to go
and the easiest, fastest route to get there.
I'm listening...

I am being divinely guided to my happiness.

I listen to my favorite music to help me reconnect with joy.

My favorite music is medicine for my soul. I use it as a tool for lifting my mood and enhancing my happiness in any moment. The frequency of a good tune lifts me to higher places of bliss, excitement, and enjoyment!

My secret to happiness is radical acceptance.

When I choose to accept myself fully—as I am—and embrace my life unconditionally—exactly the way it is—I feel much happier. There is no need to fight, protest, or push against anything. Now I can just be. Radical acceptance helps set me free.

*I am much stronger
than my excuses.*

When my mind conjures up reasons why I
shouldn't be happy, I overcome those doubts
and fears with unwavering grace. I know
I deserve to be happy no matter what.

I can!

I can feel good more often. I can be happy
if I want to. I can create a good life for
myself. I can embrace more joy. I can practice
more optimism. I can be radiant. I can enjoy
more miracles. I can enjoy being me.

Everything
is unfolding
for my highest
good.

Just as the tides ebb and flow, so does my mood.

Without force and without manipulation, I simply observe my ever-changing mood and know that it flows just like nature, because I am a part of nature. My emotions, like the tide, never stay stagnant for too long, and knowing this helps me to relax and go with the flow.

I am learning how to be happier.

I'll admit that a part of me hasn't known how to create happiness for myself. I forgive myself for expecting to be happy without knowing how to actually do it. I am willing to learn what it really takes to make me happy and start doing more of that!

Happiness
is my gift to
myself.

Forgiveness opens me up to more happiness.

Forgiveness is first and foremost a gift to myself. As I set myself free from the trap of resentment, which ironically blocks my happiness and nobody else's, I am opened back up to experience more happiness and peace.

When I'm happy, anything is possible.

I owe it to myself to try to create more happiness because I'm at my best when I'm happy. When I'm happy, I radiate love and light. When I'm happy, I'm a powerful creator!

I ask for help when I need it.

My life is not meant to be lived alone.
Community and connection are natural,
beneficial, and, at the end of the day, crucial
to my well-being. Therefore, I let people in
and accept people's help. I welcome support
for my happiness.

I offer help when I can give it.

Helping others brings a special kind of joy that cannot be accessed in any other way. When I fill the cups of others, I simultaneously fill my own. Giving is living, and I can't help but smile when I do it!

Happiness is a state of mind that I can access anytime.

I allow myself to see the miracles all around me.

Every breath I take is its own tiny miracle. I'm ready to start noticing these miracles in my daily life so I can give this life the proper thanks that it deserves. It's a miracle to be alive! What more do I need to be happy?

Joy is something I can practice.

Most times, joy is a gift that's here when it's here and not when it's not. But perhaps joy can be practiced until it becomes my most natural state. Perhaps I can decide to feel good and keep practicing this feeling over and over. After all, my life is my choice. Why not choose joy?

Smiling feels nice. I think I'll smile more today!

It's all right to take care of myself first sometimes.

There is a reason why flight attendants always suggest that I put on my own oxygen mask before assisting anyone else in an emergency. What good am I to others if I don't feel well myself? I give myself permission to assist myself first. I deserve my own love and attention too.

Being around water helps me connect with my flow.

I look to the elements of nature to model sustainable peace and well-being for myself. Just as water flows and changes shapes, so do I. Accepting and embracing my own flow helps me to release resistance and embrace more freedom.

Happiness is a seed that I'm nurturing inside me.

With every happy thought, every beneficial choice, and every supportive habit, I am encouraging my happiness to grow. Just as plants nourished with water and sunshine get bigger over time, my happiness grows with the right loving nourishment.

I only include things in my life that support my happiness.

If it doesn't bring joy, happiness, or support to my life, it's out! It's time to do a little spring cleaning and let go of whatever (or whoever) is no longer serving me to make space for my highest good. Goodbye, baggage....Hello, happiness!

Gratitude connects me to a profound sense of joy.

I look to things outside of money to support my happiness.

It is not money's function to make me happy, nor does it even have the ability to do so. Instead, I'm shifting my focus to look toward myself for the sacred responsibility of my own state of mind. This is the way. My ability to be happy is mine to claim.

My joy is a gift to the world.

My well-being and the pursuit of uncovering its totality are agents for positive change, not only in my life but also in everyone's lives around me. When I'm happy, I inspire and awaken the happiness in others. I trust that my well-being is an agent for positive change.

My willingness to feel good is a superpower.

It's always much easier to stay in my comfort zone, but I'm not choosing that anymore. I'm willing to feel better than ever before, and I have the courage to evolve and expand into my best self.

There are
one million
different ways
to be happy.

Like a flower, I am blossoming.

The more I turn my attention inward, the clearer I can see my true nature growing inside me. The more I encourage my happiness, the more it blossoms for me.

It brings me great joy to realize how perfect I am.

I'm becoming aware of how perfect, complete, and whole I already am. My divine perfection is a true source of joy. As I recognize the divine perfection in myself, I start noticing it in other areas of my life too!

Happiness is a vitamin for my soul!

As I wind down, I remind myself of my blessings.

As I prepare to sleep, I focus on all that I
have to be thankful for. This process helps
me sleep with a happy heart and wake up with
a fresh perspective! How I end each night is
how I will start each day. Knowing this,
I take time to do it right and set myself
up for success.

Listening to my own heartbeat reminds me of my resilience.

No matter what life throws at me, it's safe
to say that I'm stronger and more resilient
than I give myself credit for. Listening to the
beating of my heart helps me remember
this truth and believe in my ability to always
keep getting back up.

When I feel overwhelmed, I stop and simplify.

Where clutter feels heavy, simplicity elicits bliss. From now on, I'll work toward simplifying my life in any way I can. I'll simplify my to-do list, my routine, my home, and my responsibilities. Simple feels nice.

In deciding to be joyful, I demonstrate my commitment to be uplifting.

Knowing I'm meant to bring joy to everyone increases its presence within me. Being and spreading joy is my purpose, and I accept the challenge with honor and delight. I'm willing to give up whatever pettiness and negativity that stands in my way.

I'm always on the lookout for wonder and delight.

Evidence of wondrous things isn't hard to find when I'm focused on finding it! There's nothing more fun than the search for happiness in the little things.

Genuinely happy thoughts are nourishing for my soul.

How do I want to feel today?

Today I get to set myself up for success by setting the intention of how I would like to feel. First I decide, and then I figure out how to get there. It's so much easier to feel good when I have clear intentions and a simple road map!

Perfection is not my goal;
happiness is.

I don't just "save" happiness for when
circumstances seem perfect; I can choose
to enjoy it at any time. Most of the time,
things aren't as perfect as I would prefer.
But that's okay. I can still be happy!

I can adapt to any situation.

My ability to adapt translates into long-term happiness because I never get too attached to outcomes or having to have things a certain way. I'm always able to shift and expand into new realities. This gives me the freedom to keep re-creating happiness for myself no matter what.

My inner radiance can shine through anything.

No matter what happens, the light of my soul is bright enough to shine right through! My inner joy, peace, and wisdom are always close by and ready to support me through my life journey so that I can always feel free and shine bright.

My joy is exponential and limitless!

I allow all my feelings to have a voice in order for me to be truly happy.

My happiness is a feeling that can coexist simultaneously with any other feeling. Therefore, I do not need to suppress any emotion to feel better. I let all my emotions live; I give them all a voice, and this is what ultimately sets me free!

My passions lead me to happiness.

When I let my passions flow through me,
I experience powerful energy and, ultimately,
live a much happier life! My passion is
valuable because it lights me up and brings me
great pleasure. I honor it for bringing
so much joy to my life.

I breathe out stress and breathe in joy.

Loving myself brings me great joy.

Self-love is one of the many keys to living my happiest life. I'm practicing loving myself more and more every day so that I can be happy in my own skin. I'm releasing all resistance to who I am and I'm learning how to celebrate all that I am!

The ground beneath my feet supports me no matter where I'm going.

Whenever I feel disconnected, I can always take a walk outside to reconnect to my inner peace and happiness. Getting some fresh air, moving my body, and feeling the earth beneath me is an easy way to soothe my nervous system and feel better fast!

I tell myself empowering stories.

Because my mood is largely a product of the stories I tell myself and the meaning I assign to things, I choose to create stories that give my life positive meaning. My empowered storytelling can help me feel better about almost anything!

A cup of tea
can spark joy.

Pleasure is my purpose.

One of my many intentions for this lifetime
is simply to experience pure pleasure and
sheer delight. That would mean that when I'm
enjoying myself, I'm fulfilling my purpose!
How fun to have a purpose that has no end
destination or tangible goal in sight.

Bliss is never more than a thought away.

No matter how I am feeling, I can always reach for a thought that brings me some sense of relief and moves me closer to bliss. I'm learning how to soothe myself back to this wonderful state of peace. And when I can't do it alone, I simply ask for help.

I'm exactly where I need to be.

I never need to worry that I'm on the wrong path. If I needed to be somewhere else, I would be. I'm right on track! It makes me happy to know that I can never be out of alignment with my destiny, because I'm always exactly where I need to be.

It's time
to do what
makes my soul
happy.